SEO 2017

SEARCH ENGINE OPTIMIZATION FOR 2017

Dr. Christopher Nash

TABLE OF CONTENTS

INTRODUCTION

SEO is an important part of your marketing and advertising campaign. While it should not be the only thing you concentrate on, it is something that is becoming even more prevalent thanks to the advent of the internet. Without SEO, you will spend a lot of time working on a website and none of your customers will be able to find it.

There are a lot of things to consider with SEO. All of the search engines have slightly different formulas that are used to determine if a website should be ranked first or last, but none of them are handing out the rules. This is to prevent people playing the system and trying to get better rankings with a bad website. To make it more confusing, search engines frequently change the way they decide rankings, so you need to constantly change up the way your website works.

This guidebook is going to spend some time looking at SEO in 2016 and how it can affect your business website. There are a lot of topics discussed in this book to help you get started. Some of these topics include:

- An introduction to SEO—this is great for the beginner who needs some help understanding what is going on in the digital world.

- How a search engine operates—without this information, it is almost impossible to figure out what SEO options will work.

- How customers interact with search engines—this helps you to bring in the customers and get those results you are looking for.

- Why you need to spend time with search engine marketing—without it, your page is lost and you won't find any customers.

- Performing keyword research—this is probably the single most important thing you will do during your SEO marketing. Without a good keyword, your potential customers will never find you.

- Other factors that will influence your SEO—these include linking, good content, and how well the user likes your website.

- Linking and how the right links can make a big change on how well your website does

- Myths about search engines—believing the wrong statements can really harm your website so we spend some time debunking the common ones.

- Spam—search engines don't like spam and you should work to avoid the spam as much as possible.

- Tracking your success—having a good system in place for tracking your results will help you to determine if one thing is working or if you need to try a new tactic for success.

- Top tips to use in 2016—these will help to give you a leg up on the competition when it comes to SEO.

With this information, it is much easier to see some great results with your SEO. While this is not always the easiest process, it is one of the most productive when you want to turn something into a great revenue source for your business.

CHAPTER 1: AN INTRODUCTION TO SEO

Before we get too far into the tips that you will need to begin growing your business online, we need to look at what search engine optimization is and how it can be beneficial to your business. In this chapter, we will look at the definition of this important term, one you will be hearing all over the place as your business grows, why you must have SEO for your website, and some of the ways that you can do SEO to see the best results.

WHAT IS SEO?

SEO is a part of marketing that will mainly focus on growing your websites visibility in search engine results. When a potential client goes onto Google, Bing, or one of the other search engines, you want them to be able to find you, preferably in the very first search result, but within the first page is necessary. SEO works to ensure that your customers find you through various keywords that are associated with your business. When the client finds you, they can go onto your website and can make a purchase; without SEO, your website is nonexistent and your clients cannot find you at all.

SEO is a broad term that is meant to encompass both the creative and the technical elements that are needed to help increase the awareness, drive traffic, and improve your rankings on a search engine. SEO is a simple idea, but making it work can be more complex. For example, the words you place on your website can sometimes determine whether a search engine will rank you high or low for a specific keyword. Linking to other websites, keyword density, and ease of use of your page can make a difference as well.

Why do I need SEO?

Many website owners feel that SEO is a waste of their time. They think that the quality of their products and their loyal customers will be enough to keep their website relevant and doing well. But honestly, some of the worst products are ranked high in search engines, and without proper SEO, your quality product will become lost and your loyal customers will not be able to find you.

Most of the traffic on the web will be driven by a few commercial search engines including Yahoo!, Bing, and Google. While it is possible to get some traffic from social media and direct links, most of the time customers will find your website using one of these major search engines. The engines are really unique because the visitors on them are considered targeted traffic, or people who are already looking for the product you offer. Basically, the customer will put in where they want to go, and the search engine is going to bring them up a map listing all the websites that can help. If the search engine is unsuccessful at finding your website, they won't be able to show it to the customer.

Each search engine has a different algorithm that determines which websites will be placed on top. While these search engines keep the exact formula secret so that companies aren't able to cheat, this guidebook will show some things to keep in mind that allow you to have a better shot at placing well.

CAN A SEARCH ENGINE FIND ME WITHOUT SEO?

There have been a lot of advances in modern technology, but search engines are still not able to do anything. The search engine is going to need some help to find your website, and SEO is the help that gets you found. While most major search engines strive to find the best technology to get the best websites at the top of the list, their capabilities are limited.

This means that with the right SEO moves, your website can be on the top of the list, or at least within the top five. This can bring in thousands of new customers, meaning more business than you could dream possible. On the other hand, if you go about this poorly, you can become lost and all of your hard work is lost.

Basically, without performing SEO of some sort, a search is never going to be able to find you. These search engines are trying to provide a service to their customers, and if they spend hours looking for a result, the customers will go somewhere else. If you aren't ready to put in some effort with SEO and make your website appealing to the search engines, your customers will find it hard to locate you.

IS IT POSSIBLE TO DO MY OWN SEO?

In some cases, you will be able to do your own SEO. If you have run your business for some time or use the tips in this guidebook, you will find that you have some of the basics of SEO covered and could do a pretty good job. SEO education is found all around you and once you start exploring, you will find that a lot of it is pretty common sense. Just think about the things that you would look for in a website to help you out? Keep these things in mind when creating your website, and you have a pretty good shot.

In other cases, you may choose to hire a professional to help you out. There are a variety of companies who specialize in SEO and who can do the work for you. If you are low on time, are worried about how to get this work done, or you just aren't that familiar with SEO, an SEO company may be the route for you to get results.

SEO is complex, but it is basically the steps that you take to ensure that a search engine is able to find you when a potential customer is searching for you. Follow the right steps and you can be top of the list and bring in many new customers.

CHAPTER 2: HOW SEARCH ENGINES OPERATE

Without an understanding of how search engines work, you stand no chance of your customers ever finding you. Your customers will choose a certain search engine based on how easy it is to use, how relevant the results are in a search and so many other factors. Learning how a search engine makes itself appeal to your potential customers makes all the difference when it comes to ranking your website high.

Every search engine has two different functions. This includes providing a ranked list of the most relevant websites to a search user based on specific terms, and building up an index. Each search engine will perform these tasks in various ways to help make them stand out from other search engines. Let's take a look at these two kinds of functions of your search engines and how they will affect your SEO efforts.

INDEXING AND CRAWLING

First, let's make the internet into something a bit more concrete. Think of the Internet like a big subway system that has a lot of stops all connected together. Each of the stops along this subway is a different document; for the Internet, this is usually going to be a webpage but it could also be a picture, a PDF file, or something else. On this subway system, there has to be a way for the search engine to get from the home page to find the stops that are needed along the subway.

There are millions of these stops and if a webpage didn't have a system in place, you could spend hours online trying to find something you need. The search engine has put together a code to find the best available paths; these are called links. These links are going to allow the crawlers or spiders, the automated robots for a search engine, to get to all of the documents that are on the web.

Once the search engine you are using is able to find the pages, they will decipher the codes with each of them and then store this information on a big database. This makes it easier for the search engine to recall the information later when you send out a search query. While this may seem like it would take forever to recall even the simplest of information, companies that run search engines have multiple data centers throughout the world that help them to keep the information in order and offers the opportunity for you to access this information in just seconds rather than hours.

PROVIDE THE ANSWERS

When you go on a search engine, what are you looking to accomplish? Does the search engine open and just offer all the billions of pages of information available online all at once? No, that would be insane and it would take you forever to sort through it all. In most cases, you go online because you want to get a question answered. You want to find out who sells shoes in your area, how far to your favorite restaurant, find out information for your history paper, or some other information and you want the search engine to provide you with this information as quickly as possible.

In the beginning, search engines would simply look for certain words on a page and then present these as the most relevant options to your search. While this was a simplistic method to use that did turn some great results in the beginning, people quickly figured this out. Soon websites began padding their content to have as many of a certain phrase as possible, even if it really isn't the most relevant to your needs. Over time, search engines knew they needed to do more to help match the results better to what the searcher wanted, and to prevent the websites from taking advantage of the system. Now, most search engines have a combination of factors that will help determine if a website is relevant to the searcher.

To start, most search engines assume that a site, document, or page that is really popular is going to have a lot of important and relevant information to the searcher. The idea is that people wouldn't go to the page if they weren't finding the information they need. Using this can be pretty successful in providing relevant results to consumers.

The search engines won't use a manual system to determine the relevance or popularity of a site. Instead, a search engine is going to have a mathematical equation that will sort out the good versus the bad websites and then they will rank the good stuff based on how popular they are. Each search engine has their own equation for determining the relevant and popular websites and often there are many factors that can rank you higher or lower on a search engine results page. This mathematical equation helps to keep the ranking fair for all websites.

STARTING TO FIND SOME SUCCESS

Since each search engine has their own algorithm for deciding the relevance and popularity of a website and there are perhaps hundreds of factors that are determined, it can be easy to feel like you are lost in the beginning. How in the world are you going to take a brand new website and make it rank even on the first page of a search result, much less at the very top?

While it may seem like the search engines are out to get you, in reality, they just don't want companies to game the system. If they released the exact formula for how they decide who gets ranked top, everyone would just make sure their websites matched up to this formula and the searcher would get a lot of information that has no relevance to them.

But the search engines do give some hints to try and help out websites. They want you to succeed, but they want it to be in a way that helps the searcher, not in a way that lets you game up the system.

GOOGLE RECOMMENDATIONS

Google is still king when it comes to SEO. Many websites that are trying to rate high on a search engine will work with Google to see some great results. Some of the tips that Google gives for websites that want to be found by potential customers include:

- Make the pages useful to your user, and not for the search engine. Never try to deceive the user or try to present information differently to the search engine than what the user will see. This term is known as cloaking. It can harm your rankings as fewer customers will look at it and you can be kicked off all searches if found out.
- Make your site clear and organized. Use text links for organization. Each of the pages on your website should have a way to be reached by one, if not more, static text link.
- Fill your website with useful information. The pages should have text that accurately and clearly describes all your content. Keep the title descriptive as well. One of the ways that a website ranks high is because there is a lot of information inside.
- Keywords are your friends. Use these to create URLs that are human friendly and very descriptive. Use keywords that would matter to your customers and helps them to find you, but don't overstuff the content with these words too much.

BING RECOMMENDATIONS

Bing is a new search engine that is making waves as one of the best online. While it hasn't come near to the reputation Google has created over the years, Bing is considered by some far superior to the results of Google. Bing is created by Microsoft so you know you are getting some great engineers behind any result you find. Some of the tips you should keep in mind when you are trying to rank your website:

- Unsure that a keyword rich and clean URL structure is found in your website.
- Don't hide your content into some rich media. These would include things like Ajax, JavaScript, and Flash Player. Also, take the time to verify that these rich media sources aren't hiding links from the crawlers or you won't be found.
- Create content that is keyword rich and try to match relevant keywords in your content to what searchers are looking for.
- Keep the content on your website fresh as much as possible.
- Never put indexed text inside an image. For example, your company address or name should not be placed in a logo if you want it indexed.

While this isn't a full summary of everything your website needs to be ranked high in a search, it can give you a good start. If your website doesn't have some of this information, it is less likely to be found high in the rankings and your customers will not be able to find you.

Experiment in SEO

While you won't be able to get the search engines to give you a complete list of factors for ranking a website, you can get a good idea of how to design your own website with this little experiment. For this activity, we are going to make up our own website, complete a few steps, and then see how well it ranks on various search engines along with what different changes do to encourage the relevance of the website.

Step 1:

First, pick a site that you can use to create a website. Register it with some nonsense keywords. These don't even have to be real words; we want to quickly see how well the website is doing without a lot of other results in the way so having a nonsense or made up word or phrases can be perfect.

Step 2:

On the website, create several pages that are all connected, but make sure that all of the pages are targeting the same nonsense term that the website is registered under.

Step 3:

When creating the webpages, make these pages very similar, almost identical. Then on each page, alter one single variable. You can experiment with where the text is placed, how you format the text, link structures, and even the use of keywords.

Step 4:

Point the links for your domain at well-crawled and indexed pages on some of the other domains.

Step 5:

Publish your website and wait a few days until it shows up in search results. After a few days, look up the pages of your website and record how well they are ranked on their search engines.

Step 6:

Once you have recorded these findings, you should make some small alterations to your pages and then reassess how these changes have impacted the relevance of each page on a search engine. If the change makes the website go down in relevance, you may need to consider not using that particular change.

Step 7:

While this process may take a bit, the point is to figure out which variations will work the best to rank your random website high in a search engine. Write down any of the results that seem really effective and then retest a few times. Over time, you can begin to see some patterns by the search engines. Use this information when working on your actual website and you will rank higher in a search engine.

This process is not going to guarantee that you are ranked number one on a search engine, but it is going to help you rank much higher than just shooting in the dark. It is going to take some time but you can easily transfer this to your company website once the results come in. If your website happens to get ranked lower over time, go through the process again and see if the search engine has change their pattern.

If you hire a SEO company to help rank your website, they have probably gone through a process similar to this one to help you. This is usually more time effective, but you can also do this process on your own if you have the time and patience to see it through.

CHAPTER 3: THE INTERACTION BETWEEN SEARCH ENGINES AND YOUR CLIENTS

The biggest determinant of whether your potential customers is to make the information on the website relevant to them. You can't fool the search engines for long; if your customers can't find relevant information when they look for it, they won't come back to the website and won't stay around for long. It is important that you build your SEO around an idea of empathy for the audience. When you know what the target market looks for in your website, it is easier to reach and then keep this market.

STEPS CUSTOMERS USE TO FIND INFORMATION

The way customers have used search engines throughout the years has changed quite a bit. But there are still some steps that stay the same for how people search for and then find information that they need. The basic steps that are used for a search include:

1. Need to receive some sort of information. People go on a search engine when they need to find out some information. Whether they need to learn something new, purchase tickets, or get directions, there is some solution or answer the person needs to know before going on a search engine.
2. Formulate keywords. Once there is a need, the searcher will create a word or string of words describing what they want to find out.

3. Search the keywords. The searcher will place this string of words into their chosen search engine in the hopes of finding some good results.
4. Browse the results—the search engine should be able to find some results based on the phrase a searcher puts in. The searcher can then look at the results and see which one looks like it matches their needs the best.
5. Choose a result—from the results on the page, the searcher will be able to pick out a result that looks promising.
6. Scan—the searcher is going to take a few minutes to figure out if this result is going to help them. They will scan the information, look at the pictures, and even check out the headings to see if this is the best result for them. If the page looks good, they will stay there and get their information.
7. Continue searching—sometimes the website won't be what a searcher is looking for. If this is true, they will go back to their search results and look around for another link.
8. New search—if none of the websites are looking good, the searcher has the option to change their keywords and phrases and try again. Or they can begin a whole new search based on another piece of information they need.

THE POWER OF SEO TO REACH CUSTOMER

Ok, so it makes sense that people will go online and try to find out information, but how many customers are actually looking for your website or your services online? Wouldn't they just look at a store or hear from word of mouth about your services? Is it worth your time to perform some SEO to reach customers or is the market just too small?

Most business owners agree that SEO is a huge part of their whole business plan, especially when it comes to marketing. The power of SEO can ensure that your customers are going to find your website when they need your services rather than going with another competitor who put in the effort for SEO. Let's take a look at a few studies to show how much your customers are using the Internet to get answers and why SEO can make a huge difference in your business.

PEW INTERNET STUDY

This study was done in 2011 and shows how the use of search engines has increased quite a bit. This study showed that in 2002, Internet users who were on search engines on a regular day was at about 33 percent. These people would go and search for an answer to their questions or use a search engine to find a website that they need. In 2011, this number had risen to 59 percent of users using search engines and in 2015, it is believed this number has risen to over 75 percent.

These numbers are equal to if not greater than the number of internet users who are using search engines for e-mail. Since a big percentage of people use internet for personal and business use, the fact that this many people also use search engines each day is pretty large.

GOOGLE IS LEADING

A report done by StatCounter Global Stats shows that the search engine you choose to go with will also determine how many customers will choose your website over another. Some search engines get very little traffic and placing all your efforts with them will not show much increase in traffic or sales to your business. But placing that same energy with other search engines, mainly Google, can help to really increase your views and traffic. The top search engines include:

- Google—this is the king of all search engines. Over 90 percent of search engine traffic to websites comes from Google. If you are the top search in Google, you are likely to receive more than 18 percent of all search engine click through traffic. The second position will get more than 10 percent so it is worth your time to place effort on Google.
- Yahoo!—this search engine will get 3.78 percent of traffic
- Bing—this search engine gets 3.72 percent of traffic. While this search engine does not get as much percentage of traffic as Google, those who get a top ranking on Bing will get almost 10 percent click through rate.
- Ask Jeeves—this search engine gets about .36 percent of traffic
- Baidu—this search engine gets about .35 percent of traffic.

As you can see, Google is leaving everyone in the dust, which is why most SEO efforts are focused on being seen with Google. If you are able to reach a large audience with Google, you have a good chance of scoring high on the others.

According to a comScore study done in 2011, Google led the search market with over 65 percent of all searches conducted in the United States. In October, Google saw 13.4 billion searches by Americans; this is a large percentage of the 20.3 billion searches that were done on all searches combined in October.

With these high of numbers, it is great to spend your time working with Google. You are going to reach the biggest amount of potential customers with the same effort you would put in with some of the other search engines. Most SEO companies have studied and worked extensively with Google to ensure that businesses are finding their customers and really seeing results from SEO. If you do SEO on your own, make sure to concentrate the majority of your efforts on scoring high in Google.

WHAT THIS DATA MEANS

This impressive data is meant to help you understand that SEO is critical to your business. It is even more important in 2016 than it was when the Internet first began. Back in the advent of the Internet, most people were just amazed by its novelty and were getting used to how the whole thing worked. Now, consumers are smarter and they go online with a purpose. They want to be able to find their information as quickly as possible. Companies that can meet this need are more likely to get their business while the others are ignored.

What all this data means can be critical to how you conduct your SEO and how much of your time and budget should be given to SEO. Some important information about SEO you should keep in mind includes:

- The use of search engines is popular and is growing every year. Almost everyone in America who goes online will use search engines at least once in a while and it is almost as common for searchers throughout the world.

- Search engines are able to drive a huge amount of offline and online economy in ways that you are not able to do with all of your other marketing endeavors.
- To be found by potential customers, you need to be found within the first few results on a search engine, especially on Google.
- When you are listed as a top result on a search engine, you get a lot of traffic as potential customers will find your website easily. Also, being a top result helps consumers trust you and to feel that your company is important and worth their time.

In order to take advantage of everything SEO has to offer your business, you need to learn how to use SEO properly to reach your potential consumers when they need you most.

Chapter 4: The Necessity of Search Engine Marketing

Working with SEO is important if you would like search engines and users to have a chance at understanding what you are about. Of course, even though software is being developed to help search engines do a great job at ranking websites based on relevance, no search engine is going to be able to look at a website and see it the same as a human will. But when you use SEO properly, you can help a search engine do its job a bit better.

Not everything likes the idea of SEO. It's not that they feel search engines aren't providing a good service to people, they just worry that these rankings will be abused by companies to provide them with more traffic, even though they aren't very relevant to the customers needs. But the other option, building software that actually reads through each website, would take too long and with our fast paced world, no one is going to sit around long enough to figure it out.

Technology Limits of Search Engines

SEO is amazing for your business. Search engines are able to use the tools of SEO to help potential customers find your business and choose your services when you need them most. Choosing to ignore the rules of SEO can cause some harm to your business and can actually make it almost impossible for potential and current customers to find you online. That being said, search engines are just pieces of software, and as such, they aren't perfect and have some bugs to work out.

While search engines are constantly trying to work on their technology to get rid of these bugs so they can provide the best experience to their searchers, they can't do everything. Without having an actual person there to search through all the webpages personally, something that could take days rather than a few seconds at most, there are always going to be issues with this system.

PROBLEMS WITH INDEXING AND CRAWLING

The first limits that show up with the technology of search engines is that there is an issue with the crawling and then indexing of a website. Some of the most common issues that fit under this heading include:

- Online forms—a search engine is not designed to complete any online forms, including logins, contact information, and so on. If a website has some content contained within the online form, the search engine is not able to find it.
- Duplicate pages—search engines are not going to like it when duplicate pages are found. They often see this as a way to try and fool them and most search engines want your content to be original to help with rankings. But when you use a content management system, you may create several versions of the exact same page. This is not something you can necessarily control, but it can really hurt your rankings with SEO.
- Blocked in the code—in some cases, there can be some issues with the crawling directives of a website. When this is present, the search engine could be completely blocked, no matter how well the website did with following SEO.

- Link structures are poor—if the search engines are not able to understand the link structures of a website, there may be issues with the search engine reaching the content. In addition, some content may be seen as unimportant with indexing and could be ignored.
- Non-text content—currently, many search engines find that it is difficult to index websites that have a lot of media in them. This would include formats like plug-ins, audio, video, photos, images, and any Flash files. Many search engines are working on this though since this is a unique way that new businesses are presenting their information.

PROBLEMS MATCHING CONTENT WITH SEARCH ENGINE QUERIES

In some cases, the website may not be the one with the problem. Sometimes, the query that a searcher is using can make it difficult for a search engine to find the right content. Some of the most common SEO issues concerning queries include:

- Uncommon terms—if the searcher uses a term that is not common, it can be difficult for a search engine to get results. For example, if a searcher types in "food cooling units" the search engine might be confused because most people would use "refrigerators."
- Internationalization and language subtleties—this could be something like "colour" vs. "color." Both of these are technically right, but if you use one and your searcher is using the other, they may not be able to find you.
- Incongruous location targeting—this could be that you are targeting the wrong location compared to the location where your visitors are

coming. For example, if you are targeting your content for those who are in Poland, but most of your visitors are from Japan.

- Contextual signals are mixed—sometimes, your heading will have nothing to do with what you are writing about. If you talk about the best snowboards and your title is about where to go on family vacation, you can send out confusing messages to your search engine.

If you want your information to be found by search engines, you need to try and avoid these errors and perform SEO to help market your content. It is possible to have one of the best websites in the world, but if you can't meet the metrics set out by a search engine, or get your information talked about, you will find that it is difficult to get a high ranking on any search engine.

SEO is Constantly Changing

How to use SEO is constantly changing. What was used back in the 1990s would place you at the bottom of rankings now and even in the past few years, you will see some major changes to the way search engines are trying to provide quality content to their searchers.

Back in 1990, many websites were created with a lot of keyword stuffing, Meta keyword tags, and manual submissions. This was because many search engines would basically search their indexes and then pick out the websites that had the most of a particular keyword. This is what was needed to help you get a higher ranking during this time.

Over time, search engines realized this was not the best way to do things. Many companies would stuff their websites with a keyword just to be ranked the highest. Soon, searchers were receiving articles that were so stuffed with a keyword, there really was not useful information found inside. This was really frustrating when you wanted specific information and would make you spend more time online. Because of this frustration, and the fact that companies were taking advantage of the system to increase traffic, this SEO tactic can actually place you at the lowest ranking in 2016.

In 2004, another form of SEO was used. Companies would do inter-linking with other websites in order to leverage their traffic, purchase links from spam injectors, and perform link bombing with anchor text. This helped to show that they were relevant and talked about because they would be linked to a ton of other sites.

Search engines also put a stop to this over time. It was soon seen that most of these links were bought and that no customers were actually posting them. There was a lot of spam in the message boards and often people would purposely not link to anything because no one would care. While linking is still important in helping to rank a website, search engines have changed how it needs to be done before it will bring you up or down.

2011 saw the big boom of social media and many SEO companies started to use their social media accounts and vertical search inclusion to help potential customers find them and to increase their rankings more. While using social media is a great way to grow your website and to get people talking about you, some of the tactics that SEO professionals used during 2004 can actually cause a lot of harm to your SEO and rankings today so you should be careful not to overdo the work, or try to game up the system.

As new ways of communicating with your potential customers come to light, you are going to see the world of SEO change and the search engines are going to change right along with it to ensure searchers are getting the best results every time. Because of this, if you want to be competitive with your SEO, the most important thing is to avoid gaming the system and instead, concentrate more on providing quality, relevant, and useful content that your potential customer will enjoy.

CHAPTER 5: KEYWORD RESEARCH

At this point, you may feel overwhelmed. We have discussed a lot of different things to keep in mind if you want to see success with SEO. You want to be ranked high in search engine results to increase traffic, but you also have to be careful of not gaming the system that ranks you or you would lose all your hard work.

One of the best things to focus on is the keyword. When a searcher is looking for information, they will go on their chosen search engine and click on a little box. Next, they will type in a word or a phrase that is associated with the information they wish to know about. This is known as the keyword. With the right research, you can make sure that this keyword links the potential customer with your website.

If you do nothing else right with your SEO, make sure you do the best keyword research possible. If your customers are looking up Apple's to find your product and you chose the keyword Banana's, they are never going to find you. Because of this, keyword research will become one of the highest return, valuable, and most important activities you will do in order to rank your website and bring in more traffic. Ranking along with the right keyword has the ability to break or make your website, so you need to find out which keywords are high in demand in your industry.

So how do you do this? In most cases, you need to research your customers. It is not going to do you any good to get 1000 people to your website if none of them make a purchase. But if you get 1000 people to the website and 900 make a purchase, you are doing something right.

Judging Your Keyword Value

As we discussed above, the keyword means everything to your website. There are many research tools that are available with each search engine that allow you to figure out which keyword will work the best. Of course, these tools can help out but they won't tell you exactly how much traffic you can receive from searches of the keyword. In most cases, you need to have a good understanding of your website and your customer base, make some educated guesses, and run some tests, and then repeat until you find something that works. Below is some more information on each of the steps you need to take to match your website with the perfect keyword.

Ask the Questions

When picking out a keyword, you need to determine if it is actually relevant to the content on your website. You could pick the most popular keyword online at the time, but if it has nothing to do with your website content, your product, or what your potential customers are looking for, you won't make any traffic from it. Also, think about whether the searchers of this keyword are going to find what they are looking for and be happy with the information on your page if they choose you? If the keyword can answer yes to these questions, it might be a good one for you to choose.

SEARCH FOR THIS TERM AND PHRASE

This is going to give you some valuable insight because you can look to see which websites are currently ranking for your chosen keyword. You can see how the competition has been successful in helping out the customers and you can determine whether it is easier or harder to get ranked with this keyword based on the quality of content presented.

While you are looking at all the results, check to see if there are some search advertisements on the top and the right side of the results? If the keyword is considered high value, it is more likely that a search ad will be there. The more search ads that are present, the more conversion prone and lucrative keyword.

CONSIDER A SAMPLE CAMPAIGN

One way that you can ensure that you are picking out a great keyword is to run a test campaign. This is great if the website is brand new or you haven't been able to rank for a particular keyword yet. For this, you would purchase some test traffic and then see if it converts. Bing AdCenter and Google AdWords have great programs for this which can help you to see how well you will do in searches.

For Google AdWords, you would choose to go with the exact match and then point all of the traffic to go to a particular page on the website. Wait to get about 300 clicks, if not more, and then track how many impressions you get as well as the conversion rate from this information. Don't look at the numbers too early on because this is often not enough to give you a good look at how the keyword works.

USE DATA TO DETERMINE IF KEYWORDS IS THE RIGHT FIT

You will be able to use this information to figure out if this keyword is worth your time. You can look at how many people came to your site with this keyword and how many of them actually made a purchase on your site. In addition, you can even see how much money your site made from these purchase and determine how much each purchase is with the use of a keyword.

In some cases, the keyword will convert very well. You can make a great profit with this keyword and might choose to continue using it in your website to bring in more customers. On the other hand, it often will take a few keyword tries to figure out exactly what your customers are looking for. You may have to be on the third or fourth keyword before you find one that is great for converting views and making you money. Don't settle for the first one because it's easy; find the one that does the best with matching you with your potential customers.

LONG TAIL KEYWORDS

In most cases, a simple keyword, such as "dogs" is not going to be enough to get you all the views that you would like. This term is just too broad and often won't be enough to help a customer find your website. In most cases, these simple terms are only going to make up 30 percent of all the searches. The rest will be used for what are known as long tail searches. These long tail searches are going to contain many millions of unique searches. Often these are only done a few times on an average day, but when you bring them all together, they are going to consist of most of the search engine volume.

You should choose a keyword that is considered long tail. Marketers have found that these kinds of keywords are much better at converting. Most marketers feel this is because the long tail keywords are catching people later in the conversion cycle. For example, a person who goes online and looks for the term "shoes" is most likely just looking around and trying to find a style that fits them best; they are not likely ready to make a purchase. But, someone who puts in "best prices on black high heels" are ready to make a purchase and are likely to pay out money to a company that meets their needs.

While you are less likely to find a customer who will type in the second keyword, these people are pretty much ready to make a purchase. Your conversion rate is higher and your likelihood of making a profit greatly increases. This keyword also makes you stand out from the competition more so the customers is likely to make this purchase with you rather than someone else.

Keywords are the best way to ensure that customers are going to find you. You need to be willing to stick it out with your website and your keyword for some time. There are a lot of businesses that have been around for many years. They have lots of views and are popular, making their ranking well worth all that effort.

As a beginner, you will find it is difficult to beat out these competitors when you are just starting out. But when you chooses the right keywords, provide some high quality content to your customers, and learn which keywords mean the most to your potential customers, you can slowly start to build up your ranking to be one of the firs on a search engine page.

What Keywords Work for Me?

The keywords that work the best for your website will be different than what works for another website. This is because each of you are targeting different people and may offer a new product. Some of the things that you should consider when you pick out a keyword for your website include:

Product you sell

If you are a company selling a product, you need to determine the category of product. Be more specific than "shoes" or "animals." Thousands of other sites sell these same things and it can be almost impossible for you to get ranked when competing against some of the bigger companies in the beginning. Find something that is unique with your product and find a phrase that would be easy for customer to remember and choose when doing a search online.

You can keep this same thing in mind when you are just writing important information that someone would be interested in. Treat your writing as a product and pick keywords that are popular in your written piece or that relate to the topic at hand. Since the customer is not able to make a purchase, you need to show the value of your writing even more than some other companies.

Your target customer

As a business, you should already have a good idea about your target customer. You should know about the age group you want to reach, what they like to do for a hobby, and even what they like to do in their free time. This is something that you did way back in your business plan and if you did this properly, you could probably walk into a grocery store and pick out a handful of people who would love your project.

Now you need to take this information with you when picking out a keyword. What would your customer type into the search engine box when looking for your product? What are they trying to find online when they look for your product? These are important questions when you want to pick out the perfect keyword that will match your customers with you and get you higher traffic numbers.

What your customer wants

To reach your customer, you need to match up your website to their needs. You need to think about the customer and what they will be looking for when they search for your product. Once you can get into the mind of a customer and answer the question about what will give them value on your website, it is much easier to pick out a keyword that will lead them directly to your business.

Information from your research

Never pick out a keyword without doing some research. While this may seem to save you some time, it can really harm you in terms of ranking well or getting people to make a purchase. This is because you are easily choosing a keyword that has nothing to do with your product or one your customers are just not using.

It is best to go through and do at least one, if not more, campaigns on a keyword. This is the best way to see which words are going to work the best for your particular product and website. If one thing does not work well, you are still saving some time in the long run and can try out something else until you see some results. Never go with a keyword that performed poorly, no matter how well you might like it, because you aren't going to get those conversions, and conversions equate to profits.

Picking out a keyword for your website can be a lot of work. You have to perform the right research and take the time to ensure your website is seen by the customers who need it most at the right time.

Chapter 6: Unexpected Factors that Influence Your SEO

We have spent some time talking about some of the main factors of SEO. Following these factors can increase your chances of ranking high up on a search rather than getting lost in the crowd. But the factors we discussed before are not the only things you should remember when you want to make an impact on your audience. Some of the other factors that your website must demonstrate to a search engine to get ranked higher include content on the website, user experience, and usability.

All search engines work to show the best results to their searchers. They work to make better software and to find the best results in just a few seconds. Of course, the idea of being the best can be subjective and the search engines can't always get it right, the engineers behind search engines make formulas that help bring up pages that are more likely to provide some value to their searchers.

The formulas used by each search engines are going to vary. Each has their own formula that is kept secret from others; this is to prevent other search engines from stealing their ideas and so websites aren't created to game the system. In general though, a few things that factor into your search engine rankings include:

- A website that is well-designed and which is going to be easily found by modern browsers.
- Easy to understand, navigate, and use,

- A website that can deliver credible, legitimate, and high quality content. Most also look for unique content that is not stolen from elsewhere.
- A website that provides direct as well as actionable information that is relevant to the original query.

Despite how great the technology might be, search engines have not figured out how to watch a video, view images, or understand text in a way similar to how humans do it. Because of this, search engines are going to decipher and then rank content based on some Meta information, in some cases this can be Meta tags but this is not a requirement, about how people are interacting with a site to help determine if a website is high quality.

Usability and the User Experiences

The experience that your searcher gets when coming to your website, and how easy your site is to use can make a big difference in your rankings. If your searcher comes to the site and the links don't work, the website is slow to load, or the searcher is not able to find anything because the page is a mess, your usability failed. But, if the page works quickly and your user is able to find things quickly, and perhaps even enjoys some of the graphics or fun stuff you put on the page, you can rank higher because of user experience.

There are only a few variables that a search engine will take into account directly when they determine ranking. This includes things like site structure, links and keywords. However, through using linking patterns, machine learning, and metrics of user engagement, a search engine is about to use intuition to figure out a particular site.

Both the user experience and the usability of a site are going to help a search engine determine if the site is high quality. While this may be an indirect route to rankings, it can usually do a good job at figuring out which sites people like and which ones are going to be considered a waste to the consumer's time.

This means that if you want to be ranked high in a search engine, you need to create a stellar site. You want to provide the exact information your clients want in an organized manner. If you have more than one page on your website, make sure that all the links work and that your searchers are able to get around the website without issues. When searchers enjoy the site and find what they want, they are more likely to go through inbound links, make return visits, bookmark your site, and even share the website to bring in more customers.

QUALITY CONTENT

So in order to get the search engine to rank you highly, you need to provide content that looks good and helps out all searchers. The search engine is going to be able to check through your webpage to decide if quality content is present and how good that content is compared to other similar pages. Some of the signals that a search engine is going to look for in terms of quality content include:

ENGAGEMENT METRICS

When you type in a search online, the search engine is going to brig you several results that may match up. It is then going to figure out if it's successful with the rankings based on how you are engaging with these results. If you go into the first link, but only spend a few seconds on the page before going out and trying out the next link in line, the search engine is going to assume that you are not happy with this first result. If a lot of searchers begin to quickly exit a webpage, the search engine will start to notice and may start ranking that one further down since it doesn't appeal to searchers.

Search engines want to make sure that a search is getting a long click. This long click is basically where the user will click on a website and spend at least a few minutes there rather than going right back to a search results. The longer a searcher is on a site, the more valuable the information is considered.

Search engines are going to do this millions of times each day. Over time, there is a pretty good data pool of information that helps the search engine decide if a site needs to be moved down or another one moved up based on how the searcher was able to interact with it.

Machine Learning

Back in 2011, Google was able to introduce an update known as Panda. This update was meant to help the search engine do a better job judging the quality of a website. This program was supposed to mimic the way that humans were interacting with websites. In tests, Google hired evaluators to go through thousands of different sites and then rank them based on the content. This was all done manually by humans to figure out what was considered good and what was bad content. After the test was done, machine learning was used to mimic the results of the evaluators.

After some time, the computers became fairly accurate at judging if a site was high or low quality similar to how a human would judge the site. This ended up changing the rankings of a huge amount of sites when the update first came out. It is believed that more than 20 percent of the search results with Google were rearranged thanks to this new formatting. The update was much better at figuring out what a searcher would value or want to use to answer their questions compared to the formula Google was using before.

Linking Patterns

When it comes to the internet, linking is the equivalent of a popularity vote. This means that the more links your website can get, the higher ranking you will receive. Of course, you need to make sure the links are legitimate and you aren't paying for links. Search engines have complex formulas in place meant to prevent companies from just placing links all over the place without someone actually seeing this information.

CRAFTING CONTENT

So what this all means for your business is that you need to make sure the content of your website is high. Don't just write out a page with some keywords in the hopes of trapping customers or tricking them into purchasing your product. Consumers are smart, and many of them can spend five seconds on your site before determining it is not worth their time. If this happens with a lot of searchers, your number one ranking can quickly go down.

When crafting content, think about how it can affect the customers. Will they find it useful in answering their questions? Is the content laid out in a manner that makes it easy to read and to get around the website? Would you spend much time on the website, looking around and reading the information? Keeping the content clean and useful, and ensuring that the searcher has a nice time on your website can help to keep your rankings high.

THE FLAVORS OF SEARCH INTENT

When it comes to searches, each searcher is going to have something different in mind when they come online. Some want to make purchases and will want to find a website that has their product and is easy to navigate around. Others would like to go right to a particular website; they may know the name of the website and go straight there, or the URL name is unknown so they will type in keywords to get right there. Or, some searchers want to find out information, such as topics for a history paper or to hear the news for that day.

While all of these are commonly used topics for a searcher to go with, each of them are going to take a different content type in order to attract in the searcher. If someone is going to make a purchase, they are probably more interested in pictures and prices compared to someone who is looking for information on WWII who would rather have a lot of well-designed information on the page.

The three types of content you might have to consider when it comes to attracting searchers to your page include:

- Transactional searches—these are searchers where the searcher will want to complete a task, make an online purchase, or try to find a local business. You don't need to have a credit card to sign up for these kinds of searchers. You can fit under this category if you try out a free trial, make a Gmail account, or even look for the best steakhouse in the area.
- Navigational searches—for this kind of search, someone either already knows the websites name, or has an idea of how to find a particular website. They are planning on going directly to this website to get everything they need. Even if they type in the keyword, they are probably going to find the result right on top and not search around any more.
- Information searchers—these searches include ego-searching, getting an answer quickly, or getting information that is non-transactional. Under this search, you can get directions to a new location, check out the weather, or just learn something new.

Your website is going to fit into one of these categories. You need to figure out which one works the best for your needs, and then fit the content around what you need. Try to find a way to present the information so it looks good to the searchers, but still gives them what they want. For those trying to purchase something, a website with lots of options and pictures is perfect, but if you are trying to find out information on Mars, written facts with bullet point headings is going to be preferable.

Chapter 7: Bringing in Links to Increase Your Popularity

When talking about the internet, links should be seen as streets that connect pages. Search engines want to see how many different pages are connected on these streets and whether a particular website has a lot of different links connected to it.

Ever since the 1990s, search engines looked at links like a vote to determine how important or popular a particular website is. The engines have changed the way that they view these kinds of links in order to prevent websites from abusing the linking system. For example, there was a time when a website will go through and place their own links on message boards or pay for a website to link back to them. This is not allowed because it games up the system and can effectively put horrible website at the top of a search engine rankings.

Of course, links are not the most important thing when it comes to SEO, but there is some importance to this and making sure your SEO marketing has some linking in it can help make the difference between being ranked #5 and ranked #1. Let's take a look at some of the strategies you can use in order to see some success with your links.

Link Signals

Search engines have their own special formulas meant to help assign how valuable a link is. You will find that having a link to a top ranked website is going to do more for your ranking than being linked to a website that is number 200. While the link might be the same, the search engine is going to see this in a different way.

Of course, search engines carefully guard their formulas and won't give out this information willingly, but we can make some educated guesses with analysis, experience, and even testing. You may want to play around with getting links to see what is the most successful at getting your website ranked.

Global Popular

The more important a particular site is, the more any links you can associate with this website is going to matter. Take a look at Wikipedia. This website has thousands of different sites that link directly to it, showing to a search engine that it is really important and popular. Type in a search on some historical or scientific matter, and Wikipedia is likely to be one of the top searches you find.

To earn the trust that you want with a search engine, you need to form some strong links with various partners. It is always better to go with a site that is popular because this is going to give you more clout.

Let's look at it a different way. You want to start a fundraiser to help out children without coats at your school. The more people you make aware of this fundraiser, the more likely you can gather the coats and money needed to make this a success. Who do you go to first to make a big impression?

One choice is to go with the one person in class who already works with those in need. You see them going to the soup kitchen, and doing fundraisers like this. They are a great person and a guaranteed link to help you, but their circle of friends is not very big. While they are important, you are probably not going to make a big splash working with this person and will have to do more footwork to get the amount of notice needed for this cause.

The best choice is to go with someone from the "popular" group or someone who seems to have the most friends. You take the time to talk to this person, give them your point of view, and hopefully help them to go over to your cause. If you are successful, you not only got this one person, but you most likely got all their friends as well who will link up with you. Now that you have this large group, you are getting notice. Others want to see what the big deal is about and will come to at least hear about your fundraiser, and possibly donate as well. This will hopefully snowball until you've reached everyone at your school. Linking works in much the same way; go for a popular site and get a lot of great views.

Local and topic specific popularity

The Teoma search engine was one of the first who came up with the idea of local popularity. This search engine came up with the idea that getting links that are from the same community in terms of topics is much more important than getting a link randomly placed on a big website. For example, if you sell dog houses, you should get more points for getting a link on the Society of Dog Breeders website compared to putting this same link on a website that is all about roller skating.

This idea grew and is now used by a lot of different search engines. In most cases, you not only need to find a top website to link with to increase rankings, but you also need to try and keep with something in your genre. Not only does this help the search engines rank you, but it makes sure that those clicking on the links are more likely to purchase your product or find interest in the information.

Trust ranks

Each year the internet is being used, more spam comes around. Many companies try to use tactics that are not always the most honest in order to convince you to click on their site. Some can be dangerous to deal with and can place harmful material on your computer. Search engines try their best to avoid these spam so that you can actually get websites that matter to your search rather than getting a website of someone who has learned how to play the system.

When you are linking to other websites, you need to make sure they are reputable sites. Linking to a site that is believed to be untrustworthy is going to harm your site and can be hard to recover from. The higher the trust ranking of the other website, the better you will do if you can share links between each other.

Freshness

Links are not going to stay good for a long time. Some websites will go out of business, not have fresh content, or could change their names. This means that a site that may have been popular at one time is now going to go stale and it will no longer get the new links it wants. This is why you can't just get 100 links in the beginning and then stop the work. If you are going to use links, you need to keep getting new and relevant links aver time. Most search engines have some kind of freshness signals in place to see how long it has been since you got some of your popularity votes.

Social sharing

Social media has made a huge difference in the way that information is shared online. Many times you can get links to your business and website shared on various social media including Google+, Facebook, and Twitter. These kinds of links are going to be treated a bit differently compared to some of your other link choices, but they will still get you noticed. Right now, these kinds of links are not thought to have a big impact, but over time, they will probably start to matter more as social media expands.

BASICS OF LINK BUILDING

Learning how to place links on the right websites at the right time is almost like an art form. You have to understand how SEO works and really find the sites that are worth it to you. Some find that this is too much work and simply encourage their customers to share a link or spread the word while others will see this as a valuable part of their SEO and will spend a lot of time on it. This is always one of the hardest things that you need to do with SEO, but it can be the one thing that tips you over to a top spot.

Every time you work on a link campaign, you will take a different approach to getting the work done. Each product presents itself for a different method of using links and what worked well for one campaign will not always work for another product. Here are three different ways that you can acquire links to see some results.

Editorial links

These are links that are given almost naturally by pages and sites that want to have their links on your company or content. These are not going to ask for a lot of action through SEO besides creating material that is high in quality. You also need to be able to create some great awareness about your content to make the links worthwhile.

Manual link building

In your campaign, you will create links like this when you want to use SEO that emails bloggers to get links, pay for listings of some kind, or you want to submit to a directory of a site. This is going to create some kind of proposition of value because you will need to explain to the target of the link why they should create the link. You need to convince them this is in their best interests to help you out.

Self-created

There are hundreds of thousands of different websites that offer visitors who look through them the opportunity to create their own links with user profiles, blog comments, forum signatures, signing guest books, and more. These are not going to offer a lot of value when it comes to search engine rankings, but they will have some benefit if done in the right way.

If you are going to use these kinds of links, do so with caution. If you pursue this too aggressively, it is more likely you will become penalized by the search engine and not see the ranking results that you would like.

Link Building Campaign—How to Get Started

Starting a link building campaign can take a lot of time and work. But if you are able to do this in a successful manner, you will be able to find great results when you do it correctly. This is going to be a difficult thing to do, search engines won't tell you exactly how link building can help or harm your rankings and it is easy to make things go wrong. Some of the things that you need to do during your link building campaign includes:

- Ranking of search terms—take a look at some of the relevant search terms associated with your keyword. You can take the top results on this page and try to convince them to link with your website to get better results.
- MozRank—if you want to make sure you are getting all the top pages associated with your business, you need to check out MozRank. This website is going to show you how popular certain web pages are at a given time. Most of the time, those pages that have a MozRank score are going to have better rankings with search engines.
- Competitor's backlinks—take a look at all the inbound links of a competitor's website and see how well they are doing with certain keywords. You will be able to get a lot of valuable information about these links that you can do with your own website.
- Link number—the more links on a page, the more diluted their impact. While there might be a great website associated with your produce, you will find that a website with a lot of other links is not going to provide as much value to you because of the number of links.

FIVE GREAT LINK BUILDING STRATEGIES

So now that you have done a little bit of research to find out how to use links and keep your website relevant, it is time to pick out the strategy that will work the best for your needs. Of course, each business and product is going to have a strategy that works the best for them. Take the time to look at the following link building strategies to see which one works the best for your needs.

Ask customers to do linking

If you have a loyal customer base, or some partners that you work with often, you can use this to your advantage with your links. Send out some partnership badges, icons that are going to link right back to your site, similar to what is done by Google with an AdWords program. Ask them to post these on any forum boards they visit or to share with their friends. Sometimes you can get this done just by asking them to accomplish this task, other times you may need to consider making it a contest or adding some incentive.

Do a blog

A blog is a great way to provide some new content to your website on a regular basis. It can encourage the customer to come back, more than once, in order to see what new information you are writing about.

When writing a blog, it needs to be relevant and well thought out. It is never a good idea to just write nonsense or blogs that are not placed well together. You need to create an entertaining blog that has something to do with your product to ensure it shows some interest to your customers. For example, if you have a website for dog food, you should not write about gardening, politics, and going to school. Instead, write about different dog breeds, the best places to travel with a dog, and the best treats for your dog.

Also, keep the blog up to date. Try to put an article up once a week if not more. This helps to show the search engine that the website is still relevant and brings back the customers to hear more news.

Creative content that encourages viral sharing

If you have really good content, your work is done for you. People like to share funny, outrageous or unbelievable things with their friends and family; if you are able to really impress them, they want to help you to share the news without even being asked. Some examples that you may want to look at to see how you can create quality content that goes viral include the video "How Not to Clean a Window."

This can take some time to create, but you are going to love the results. People will share this information without you having to ask. If you aren't good at creating this kind of content, consider hiring someone who will be able to help you out. There are lots of designers, writers, and others who have experience with this part of SEO and who can help you to get started.

Newsworthy

If you are able to get the attention from news media, bloggers, and the press, you are going to do better with your links. People all over the place will want to link back to the original content, your website, to use as a source and to help their readers find this information. This is not always possible with your product, but if you do a big promotion, give something for free, start up something that seems to create a controversy, or even release a new product, you might be able to get the news outlets on your side and helping you out.

PAYING FOR LINKS

It is normally not a good idea for you to pay for links. While this might seem like a good way to get your name out there and to increase rankings, therefore increasing your overall sales, you will find that many search engines are trying to stop this practice. In fact, there are measures in place with many search engines that will severely penalize you for paying for links. If you are found out, your rankings go down and you are going to have wasted a ton of money.

When it comes to links, you have to know what you are doing. This is not an easy process to go through and can take a lot of time and effort. But once you get the hang of the idea and you are able to do this method properly, it can be a fantastic way to help you see results and increase your rankings.

CHAPTER 8: MYTHS ABOUT SEARCH ENGINES

As search engines have changed over time, many myths have come up as well. Many people believe these myths are rules that they can follow to get ranked highly, but then they are really surprised by the results when it is all done. It is important that you are able to separate the fact and the fiction when you are a beginner with SEO to really see some results. Here are some of the most common myths about SEO that you should understand before getting started.

COMMON SEARCH ENGINE MYTHS

Search Engine Submission

Things were factored in differently for SEO when the internet first began. During the 1990s, search engines would use submission forms as part of the equation to figure out if your site is relevant. The webmasters would just take the pages and sites with their keywords before submitting them over to the search engines. Later, the search engine would go through the whole website and then index the website.

This was basic SEO when things were first getting started, but this method didn't stay around for too long. It was too easy for spam sites to get through with this method and this made searchers feel frustrated. Because of this, the crawl-based engines eventually replaced the old versions. Basically, since 2001, it has been useless to try and use search engine submission in order to rank well in

SEO. You can do it, but you aren't going to get any points for it when it comes to ranking.

Yes, you will still see some of these kinds of websites show up in the search results. Search engines have not found a perfect formula to ensure that these things never show up. But for the most part, this is a remnant of the past and not worth your time. If you are talking to an SEO professional who wants to use search engine submission as a part of their campaign, go and find someone else because this person just wants to take your money.

Meta Tags

Meta tags used to have a big place in a SEO marketing campaign. You would place all the keywords you were trying to rank your website for, and then anytime the searcher typed in one of these keywords, it was possible for your site to show up in the search. Of course, it didn't take long for this process to add in a lot of spam. People would find the most popular keyword at the time and associate it with their website, regardless of if the keyword had anything to do with that topic. Search engines quickly dropped this, leaving Meta tags worthless.

Rather than worrying about the Meta tags, concentrate on some other important places for keywords, including Meta description tags or the title tags. While you still need to understand how Meta tags work with search engines, they are not as important for your SEO.

Keyword Surfing

At one time, it was believed that stuffing as many keywords into a website would make a lot of difference when it came to rankings. The idea was the more your keyword was present in the website, the more likely the search engine would find you and place you higher in the rankings. This worked great for awhile, until you started getting articles that looked like spam or were so full of keywords that it was too difficult to read through.

Search engines don't want all of these spam articles to show up, so the importance of keywords has changed. While you still need to have an important keyword present, you also need to remember that the article itself needs to provide some important information to the searcher. Keyword stuffing is going to get flagged by the search engine and could easily cost you your higher ranking.

Make sure that the keyword is present in your website at least a few times, but try to keep the density low. Usually one or two percent is all you will need to let the search engine find you without making it look like you are trying to spam the searcher. The keyword needs to fit naturally into the website while providing good information to the searcher.

There are still a lot of website owners who feel that stuffing keywords is the best way to see results. Stay away from these tactics. They may happen to get into a top result for a short period of time, but soon the search engine will catch up and they will disappear. If you want to get good results, give your customers a good experience, and maintain your higher ranking, you need to use the keywords smartly and avoid keyword stuffing.

Paid search

There are a lot of SEO professionals who are going to try and convince you to do a pay per click advertising in order to bolster the organic results and get some better rankings. In most cases, you will just be wasting your money. This kind of advertising is not proven to increase organic search results and with some of the major search engines, proof of doing this can rank you even further down.

While paid searches can sometimes help to find out which keywords work the best for your website or other things you can do to get better results, you will have to put in the work for a good website to ensure that the organic search results are going to come your way.

CHAPTER 9: SPAM AND HOW IT CAN HARM YOUR SEO EFFORTS

Search engines are strict against spam. They know many websites will try to trick the consumer and make them click on links that are worthless and can even harm the consumers' computer. Here are some of the things you should watch out for to ensure your website does not get considered as spam.

SPAM ON SEARCH ENGINES

No matter how hard the search engines work, you will find that spam is around. Ever since the beginning of internet, websites have tried to use spam, the practice of making websites designed to inflate their ratings or to go against the search engines to get more viewers. Spam is prevalent because of how much revenue is at stake for being one of the top rankings on a search engine. If there are thousands of dollars at stake, it is easy to see why people want to try and beat the system and get the higher ranking.

Search engines are working to avoid the spam as much as possible. They want quality sites to get at the top of the rankings, not one that happens to know how to game the system. As time goes on, it is becoming more difficult to get away with spam and it is not worth your time for two main reasons. These include:

Not worth your effort

All searchers hate spam. They don't want to waste their time online looking at websites that have nothing to do with their search. Because of this, all search engines have some incentive to try and prevent spam to keep their searchers happy. Google has worked hard over the past ten years to try and control and also reduce the space that is all around, making it one of the best search engines compared to competitor.

Since all the major search engines use their efforts to prevent spam, it is not likely that you are going to have a chance to get the spam through to your user. The search engine is going to catch you; usually before the website is placed online, but it will be caught shortly after this time. Take the time to create a great website that has a lot of value for your company and you will have better results with your SEO.

Smarter search engines

Search engines are getting smarter. They are better at guessing what is going to happen with a website and can ensure almost to 100 percent that spam won't get in. Make sure you are creating good websites or your search engine is going to get mad and remove your rankings.

SPAM ANALYSIS

Search engines are going to work hard to make sure you aren't trying to get some spam by them. The search engine is going to look at the whole website as well as individual pages to make sure everything is legitimate. There are a few things they will look for to ensure spamming is not going on includes.

Keyword stuffing

The search engine is going to spend some time checking for keyword stuffing. This is one of most obvious and common spamming techniques. If the search engine finds that there are a ton of the same keyword on a page, you probably won't get ranked. Before trying to submit your website, go through and try to figure out how many times you use a keyword and consider cutting it down a bit.

Manipulative linking

This is another form of web spam that is pretty popular. With this method, you are attempting to fool the search engines use of links to rank pages based on their popularity. Search engines have a bit more trouble with this one because there are a variety of ways that you can do this. A few of the different techniques that you will find under this option include:

- Link exchange programs—this is when several websites will come together and share links together. Search engines are used to this kind and will usually shut them down.

- Link schemes—this is were low value and fake websites are built up just because of some link sources. Link overlap, site registrations, and other things are able to help determine if this is a tactic being used.
- Paid links—you should never pay for links when working on your website. These can be a big business, and search engines don't like that you can increase your rankings with these.
- Low quality links—it doesn't do you much good to place a lot of low quality links on your website.

Cloaking

To present a good website, you need to make sure that you present the exact same information to the search engines as a human will see when they open the website. But some spam will try to hide text behind the HTML for various reasons. The most common reasons for this is to hide a virus or other malicious software that will harm the computer of a searcher. Because of the potential for harm to the searcher, the search engine is going to take the time to make sure this does not happen.

SPAM ANALYSIS ON A DOMAIN LEVEL

Search engines have another level of analysis they will go through to make sure that spam doesn't get through. The search engine is able to go through and see the different properties and traits throughout the domain to figure out if this is spam or not. Some of the factors that the search engine will look for include:

Linking practices

Just like with an individual page, a search engine is able to go through and see the kinds and quality of links that are being sent to the whole website. It is usually pretty easy to see if a site is using some manipulative activities on a consistent manner. If you have some questionable links on your website, it is time to consider moving them off to keep you safe.

Trustworthiness

As a website, you want the search engine and your searcher to trust your website. You want them to know they can get all of the information the searcher needs and that you aren't misleading them all the time. When your business is trustworthy, you don't need to spend so much time working on SEO because you will already have the customer base. But even without an established name, you need to keep the trust.

If a search engine takes a look at your website and feels like you are trying to deceive others or that something is not right with the website, it is not going to rank your website very highly. Always make sure that your customers can trust you and will keep coming back.

Content Value

The value of your content is one of the most important things that you can do when you want to rank high and not be considered spam by the search engines. Each and every page on your website needs to provide useful information to your searcher, whether you are using it as an About Me page or your blog. If you aren't a good writer, consider hiring a professional to help you craft a great website that will keep people coming back.

Has My Website Been Bad?

Are you having trouble getting your website ranked the way that you would like? Were you highly ranked at one time but now you feel your being penalized?

Step 1: Rule it out

Sometimes it is difficult to tell if your website has gotten a penalty. Sometimes the search engines will change their formulas and something that used to be fine on your website is going to harm you. Or you may have made a simple change to your website, without realizing it that will cause an issue with your site. Before you think that you are being penalized, go through and see if some of the following might be the cause of a lower ranking.

- Errors—if you have some errors on the page, or the page is not working well, you may get a lower ranking. Use Google's Search Console to have a look at the website and see if this is the issue.
- Changes—go back through and see if any of the changes you made to your page may change the way that a search engine is looking at your content.
- Similarity—check for some other sites that are similar with backlinks like yours. See if these sites have lost some rankings due to a change in the search engine formulas and then make adjustments.
- Duplicate content—duplicate content can make it difficult to get ranked. You may need to go through and change up your webpage a bit

to ensure that you aren't getting penalized for getting the same content as another site.

If you mess around with some of these factors and your website still isn't getting a higher ranking, consider moving on to step 2.

Step 2: Flowchart your way to understanding

First, look to see if the site is still indexed. If not, or if just the homepage is indexed, your site has probably been banned. Verify this using the Webmaster Central. You will need to go through and remove all the spam and then file a re-inclusion request to see if you can be let back into the search results.

If your site is still indexed, go and check if the site is still able to rank under the domain name. If your domain name is not ranking, the issue is probably because of on-site spam like keyword stuffing or cloaking, or you have an issue with some of your links. The first think you will need to do is go through and remove all the bad links, drop the paid campaigns, and clean up the content. Then submit a re-inclusion request with a promise not to do this again.

If your domain name is still ranking, check and see how highly your page is ranking. Look for 5 or so unique terms that are in the title of the pages. Are you still ranking within the top 20? If not, you've probably had a lot of your links taken away because they are considered low value. You will need to get a re-inclusion to get the webpage back up and then go through and find some great links to help you get ranked again.

If your domain name is ranking and your unique terms are still putting you on the first page of ranking, you are probably doing just fine. It is not likely that a penalty has happened and you just need to work on the SEO a bit to get some higher quality ranking results. Writing some new blog posts, finding some new high quality links, and keeping at the process will help you to get your rankings back.

GETTING BACK ON THE GOOD LIST

Getting rid of your penalties can be an uphill battle. Most search engines won't tell you what went wrong with the website or what you can do to make the situation better. In many cases, the process to be re-included in the search engine rankings can be long and painful, and most times, the search engine will deny your request. To have the best chance of being re-included in search results is to follow these steps:

1. Register your website with a Webmaster Tools service. Bing and Google both have these for you to use. This step is going to create trust and connection for you and the search engine.
2. Look through the information on the Webmaster Tools accounts. This is going to explain the different issues that might be present in your webpage such as spam alerts, crawl warnings or errors, or a page that is broken. You may be able to find that the issue for your website has nothing to do with spam and is an accessibility issue instead.
3. Send a reconsideration request. You can do this through the Webmaster Tools. Doing this through a public forum can make the request get lost.

Submitting with Webmaster Tools will make you seem more trustworthy and you are more likely to hear back.

4. Open up with all information. If you have been spamming on your website, it is better to own up to it. Provide all the information like who sold the links to you, how you were able to get them, and all the links you've gotten. Google in particular, wants this information to help improve their formulas. If you withhold this information, the search engine is going to see you as dishonest.

5. Remove all the bad stuff. Everything you can fix, you should work on right away. Take down the links, get rid of any manipulations on the page, like keyword stuffing, and fix up the website. Have all this fixed before you try and submit a request.

6. Prepare for the wait. It is likely going to take a few months before you hear back from the search engine. There are thousands of sites going through penalization at one time and they go in order.

7. If you are in charge of a website on a big powerful brand and you need your website back up right away, it is possible to speed up the process. Consider going to a conference or event and talking to one of the engineers for your search engine. You may have to pay to get into the conference but this is a small price to pay to get your website back up and running.

Trying to spam a search engine is never a good idea. It is going to cause a lot more harm to your website and your profits than it will to anyone else. Always follow reliable and trustworthy SEO tactics and you will get the ranking results that you want.

Chapter 10: Tracking Your SEO Success

You are putting in all this work, it's important to make sure that work is doing something. Tracking and measuring your success with SEO is critical to ensuring you are getting the best results from your time. It allows you to look at the website and determine if you're work is paying off or if you're missing out in one area or another. You can never improve your website without some form of measuring the website. This chapter is going to spend some time looking at the ways you can measure the success of your SEO.

Metrics to check

Every website will have some different metrics that you should consider. Some of the metrics that almost every website can track to see if their SEO is working includes:

- Share of referring visits—you should check to see how many times a customer comes to your website thanks to the search, check out typed traffic, emails links, referral traffic, and search traffic.
- Keyword searches—find out which keywords brought in the most viewers. If one isn't doing well, consider replacing it.
- Conversion rate by keywords—which keywords were able to help you get the best results for sales? Sure, one might bring in the customers, but are they spending money?

- Pages that are receiving one or more visit from a search engine—this helps you to know which pages are getting the most views and whether your website is even indexed on a search engine.

Picking a Software

There are a number of different software programs available to help you see how well your SEO efforts are doing. Each have their benefits to helping you determine which path to take. Some of the paid software that you can consider to see some great results include Unica Netinsight, Clicktale, Mint, and Moz Analytics.

There are also some freebie sites that can do a great job as well. These would include Google Analytics, AWStates, and Yahoo! Web Analytics.

Picking out the software that will work for your business is difficult, but you need to take a look around and figure out which one is actually the best for your unique needs. Read up on some reviews and maybe give a few a try to figure out which one fits with your budget and your business.

METRICS TO MEASURE

It can be hard to optimize certain behaviors that search engines are looking for because they don't make their formulas very public. But there are some tactics that have been proven by trial and error that seem to do a good job. One of the best ways to figure out the metrics to use is by looking at the specific website you like. Each of them has their own formula, but with some of their own tools and some experimenting, you can find the option that works for you.

Google

There are a few options available with Google. The first one, Google Site Query can help you to restrict your work to just one site. This allows you to see the list of pages and how many pages are indexed just under one domain. You can then change the query parameter to find out more information and what would be useful to use on your own website.

Another option is google.com/trends. This website is helpful when picking out the keywords that will rank your website. These are constantly going to change, but you can use your Google account to go through and find out which ones seem to be the best for your particular business.

Google also has a blog search option that will be able to help you with links. This operator is not always the most useful, but this search is going to give you some high quality results that you can separate out into relevance and date range to help you out.

Bing

Bing also has some nice software that can help you get your website ahead of the game. First is Bing Ads Intelligence. This is going to have a lot of information on keyword research as well as tools to figure out your audience. This one is mostly for use with advertising, but you can use some of this to help promote your own website.

Bing IP query gives you the opportunity to look just at one IP address. This is going to show up the pages that Bing has found that match up to that IP address. This is really useful if you want to find out whether there are several pages on a shared provider or if there are different sites that will be hosted onto the same IP.

Next is Bing site query. This is just where you will restrict any queries you have to one site. This is just like the one found in Google where you can show all of the pages that are indexed for one site.

These tools are meant to help you get a better idea of what is working and what you might need to improve on. Use all the tools at your disposal to help your website get the best chance.

Applying Data

Now that you have measured the success of our website, it is time to learn how to apply that data. Your website is never going to get better results if you just look at the results and then walk away. Here are some of the best signals you should be listening to in order to apply the data and really make your website shine.

Fluctuation

Site and link query numbers are rarely going to be precise. They can change all the time so unless your numbers have gone really far down, it probably isn't too big of a deal. If you notice that the drop of links on your indexed pages is coinciding with drops from traffic drops, you might have more of an issue due to indexation from malware, hacking, or penalties. You should go through and perform an in-depth analysis of the page to see what is going on.

Falling

If you find that just one search engine you rank on is now sending you a significant lower amount of traffic, there might be some issues. Often you might be in penalty because of not following the guidelines or the search engine thinks you are spam. You can sometimes get blocked by a search engine on accident, so check out your Webmaster Tools to see what is up. Or you may find that that particular search engine made some changes to their formula and now you are not favored as highly; mess around with your site to see what is going to help you out.

You can sometimes become blocked form multiple search engines and see that your rankings fall all around. For this issue, it is likely that something is wrong with the website and the search engine is either being blocked or not allowed to index you. Check the mechanics of the website to see if this might be a problem.

Ranking fluctuations

You are going to see fluctuations in your rankings all of the time. This can happen every day so it is nothing really to worry about. Search engines change their formulas or someone else might come into the ring with something unique. Just make sure to keep using proper SEO and don't try to fool the system, and you will see better rankings again.

Metrics increase, rankings stay the same

There are a lot of website owners that assume that when they do some SEO, they are going to see some results instantly. This is not always going to happen. The system just has so many websites moving through it all the time that instant gratification is not going to happen. Even with lots of great SEO methods, it can take some time before your website moves to the top. The process of crawling the pages, indexing them, and then going through processing will take the search engines some time too.

So be patient, the search engine is going to find you and rank you well if you do your job right. But it can sometimes take a bit of time to bring it all together and to get your website the number one ranking it deserves.

Measuring your SEO is one of the best ways to determine if you are going to get all the customers you would like or if something is just not adding up right. Check your measurements often so you can make the right changes and keep your website on top.

CHAPTER 11: TOP 2016 SEO TIPS TO REALLY SEE RESULTS

We have spent a lot of time discussing how SEO can be used in your websites to ensure you are reaching your potential customers by scoring high in search engine rankings. The way that you use SEO is going to change from year to year. Search engines are always changing their formulas to try and provide the best results to their searchers and to avoid a company taking advantage of the system and placing bad results on top. Because of this, it is critical that you learn the SEO tactics that are going to help you out in 2016 to stay relevant. Let's take a look at some of the best tactics for SEO in 2016.

THE TITLE

By this point, you should have a good idea of the keyword you would like to use with your webpage. This keyword will make it easier for your potential customers to find you and should give a good description of what your website is about and what you are selling.

Many people forget that their title is an important part of the article and can be one of the best places to put your keyword when you are talking about SEO. It doesn't make much sense to have a website about a keyword, if that keyword isn't even important enough to place in the title.

When it comes to Google, the first thing that is looked at is the title. So make sure that you are wisely using the main keyword somewhere in the title. Don't try to force this though. Be careful and ensure that the keyword actually fits into place. Forcing the keyword will sound and look awkward and could lessen your chances of getting into a top ranking spot. But if you do this properly and make it flow naturally, you have a good chance of getting ranked highly.

Domain Name and Keywords

If possible, choose a keyword that would work nicely in your domain name. If you are able to do this, it is highly likely that you will be able to get the first position, or at least one that is very high, in the rankings for this particular keyword. When the keyword is available right away in the domain, it is much easier for the website crawlers to find your website and they will rank it right on top.

Domain Name Age

In this case, you want to go with a domain name that is older. Search engines like domain names that have been around for awhile. This shows that the site has gotten enough views and popularity to stay around for awhile and that the content is probably good enough to keep you around. Also, many spam sites will only go up for a few months before being found and taken down. For this reason, a domain that has been around for only a year is going to have more issues ranking high compared to one that is five years old.

What this means is that you need to stick with the work. Don't give up after just a year or so of your website. The first few years might be a bit difficult, but over time, you are automatically going to get higher rankings. Keep with this work, and you will find that it is much easier to rank higher and get more viewers.

Low Keyword Density

In 2016, it is not a good idea to try and stuff as many keywords into a webpage as possible. This is going to set up some red flags with the search engines and can make it really difficult for you to see the results that you would like with rankings.

For the best results, you should make sure to keep your keyword density to less than 3 percent. In most cases, going closer to 1 or 2 percent is the best. This helps to fit the keyword into the article a bit better without stuffing the article or making it sound awkward when the searcher looks at your page.

There are a few different tools that you can use to help determine how many times the keyword is found in an article. You should use these tools on each page or article you decide to place inside your website. If you find that the keyword is showing up too often, you should try to cut it down a bit to get the best SEO results.

WEBSITE SPEED AND MOBILE FRIENDLINESS

No searcher wants to spend forever waiting for your website to load up. If they have to wait more than a few seconds, they will probably go backwards and pick out a different website. This means that you will lose at ranking points and have trouble bringing in some more searchers later on.

So, one of the first things you should do is make sure your website is able to open and function quickly to make the searchers happy. You should make sure to keep the domain fresh and work with a company that can keep the website working properly at all times.

Another thing you should consider in 2016 is making your website mobile friendly. More and more people are starting to use other means to go through and find the information they need. Mobile phones are one of these popular methods, meaning that if your website does not work properly on many devices, including mobile devices, you are going to find it almost impossible to get a good ranking.

SITEMAP OF THE WEBSITE

When creating your website, make sure the sitemap is easy to use and well organized. The crawler's of a search engine like to go through and look at every piece of your sitemap before you become indexed. This is so the search engine has all of the pages matched up to the right keywords and can find your relevant pages faster when someone does a search that might match up with you.

If your sitemap is not in good shape, it can be really difficult for the crawler's to find your information. You may be indexed, but the information is all over the place and no one is going to be able to find you later on. Keep is organized and things will go so much better.

BACKLINKS APPROVED BY PENGUIN

Backlinks can do a lot of great things when it comes to your website. They make it easier for people to find your website and they show the search engine that you are gaining in popularity. This can be a complicated procedure, but can really help you to increase in rankings if done properly.

With the advent of Google's Penguin program, you have to take extra precautions to ensure your links are actually helping you rather than causing harm to your ranking system. Some of the things you should do to ensure you stay relevant with Google Penguin and continue seeing results include:

- Don't pay for links—never pay people to post links or go around and post your links all over the place. These are not quality links and Penguin will be able to see it quickly. Real links by your customers are going to rank you higher than anything else.
- Pick quality sites—when you want to have links back to your website, make sure you are going with quality sites. Don't pick ones that are considered spam or that have only a handful of viewers. While these sites might be really nice, placing links on these sites can harm your search engine rankings.

- Pick sites relevant to your website—while it would be nice to place links on the most visited site all the time, this does not always point out a quality link. It doesn't make sense to place links on a site for shoes if you are in the hospital market. Not only can this hurt your ranking, it will keep you away from the customers who would actually make a purchase through your website.
- Update links when needed—always keep your links updated. You don't want your indexed links to be outdated or rundown. This is going to make your rankings go down.
- Pick high ranked sites—when picking out websites to link with, make sure you are going with those that are ranked higher. This shows the search engine that you are well liked and associated with other high ranked sites, so maybe you should be ranked higher as well.

Duplicate Content Issues

Never ever take content from another source and use it as your own. Search engines like to see quality content that is unique. While you can have a similar product or story as another website, you just shouldn't use the exact same wording on your own website.

This was a problem that occurred for some time with websites. They would see that a breaking story came out, or one that was well-done and very popular, and many websites would copy the work and try to put it on their own. They may try some more linking, keywords, and other tactics in order to increase their rankings and perhaps sell a product. Soon, you would do a keyword search and find ten or more websites with the exact same article on them.

Search engines have started cracking down on this. If you try to publish duplicate content, you are not able to get a high ranking in the search engines. The search engines don't want to disappoint their users with a lot of duplicate content so always strive to make your own and make it high quality. This will bring in the viewers and ensure that you get the best ranking results.

SOCIAL SHARES

When it comes to SEO, social media can add in a lot of power. The more comments, shares, and likes you can get on your social media sites as well as with your blogs, the higher you will rank with search engines. This is because these activities show the search engine that you are really popular with users and that others are talking about you. If this group of people use energy to talk about you, it is easy to see that others would want to find your information as well, making it easier to become ranked.

When you create a blog or have a social media page, make sure to provide quality content. This is true even on a Twitter or Facebook page. Update the information often to keep consumers coming back to see your page again. It isn't going to help your rankings if you provide one great article or event that draws people in and then they never come back. But continuous good writing and content can help to keep your viewers coming back and your rankings high.

When you follow some of these easy tips, you will see great results with your search engine ranking. Just remember to pick the right keywords, produce original and quality content, and don't try to fool the search engines and you are sure to get some of the great results you have been looking for.

Conclusion

SEO is one of the most important things you can do to bring in more customers and make more profits. More and more of your customers are going online to find products and information, and the more visible you can be in this crowd, the more money you can make. But you have to follow the right formula to make sure customers are finding you.

SEO can be a challenge. None of the search engines have a list of all requirements to meet SEO and to be ranked as number one; if they did, everyone would try to game up the system. But with some research and common sense, it is easier to see what the search engines are looking for to rank you high.

This guidebook is meant to help you navigate the world of SEO, especially as we enter 2017. The rules are constantly changing, and it is important to keep up to ensure that your customers are able to pick you out of the mess. Take a look at this guidebook and see what you need to do to get started on a good SEO campaign and get your website noticed now.

www.ingramcontent.com/pod-product-compliance
Lightning Source LLC
Chambersburg PA
CBHW061018050326
40689CB00012B/2673